The Winter's Collection of

DERBY

The Winter's Collection of
DERBY

BREEDON
BOOKS

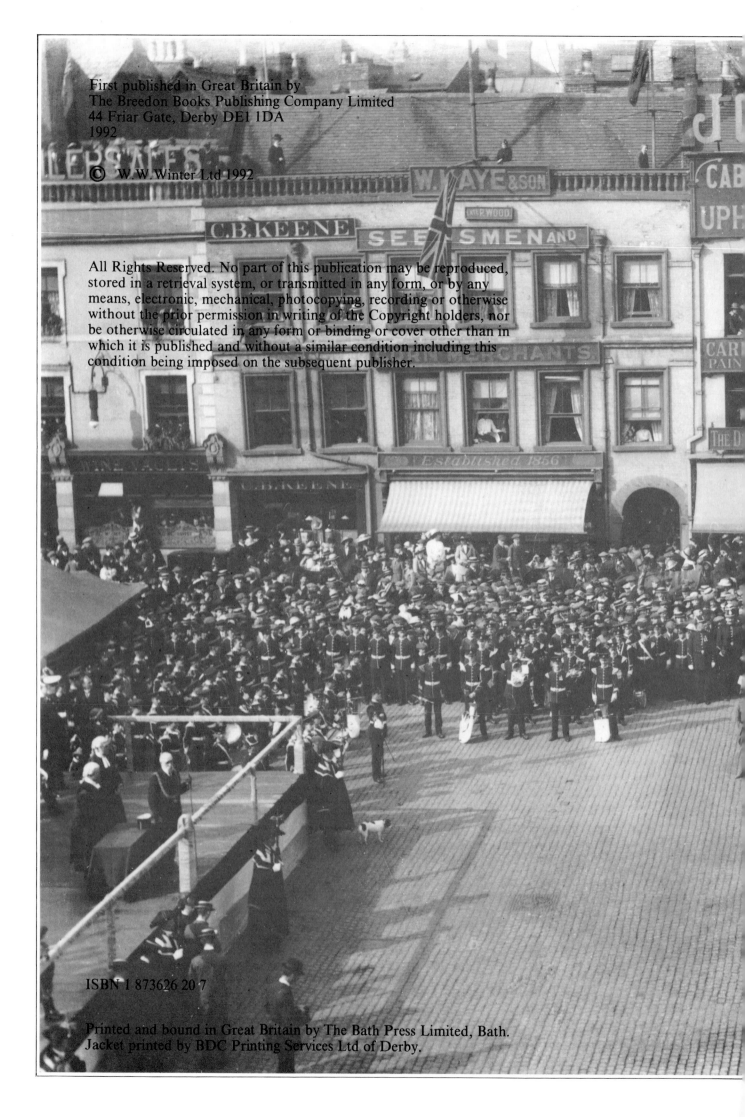

First published in Great Britain by
The Breedon Books Publishing Company Limited
44 Friar Gate, Derby DE1 1DA
1992

ISBN 1 873626 20 7

Printed and bound in Great Britain by The Bath Press Limited, Bath.
Jacket printed by BDC Printing Services Ltd of Derby.

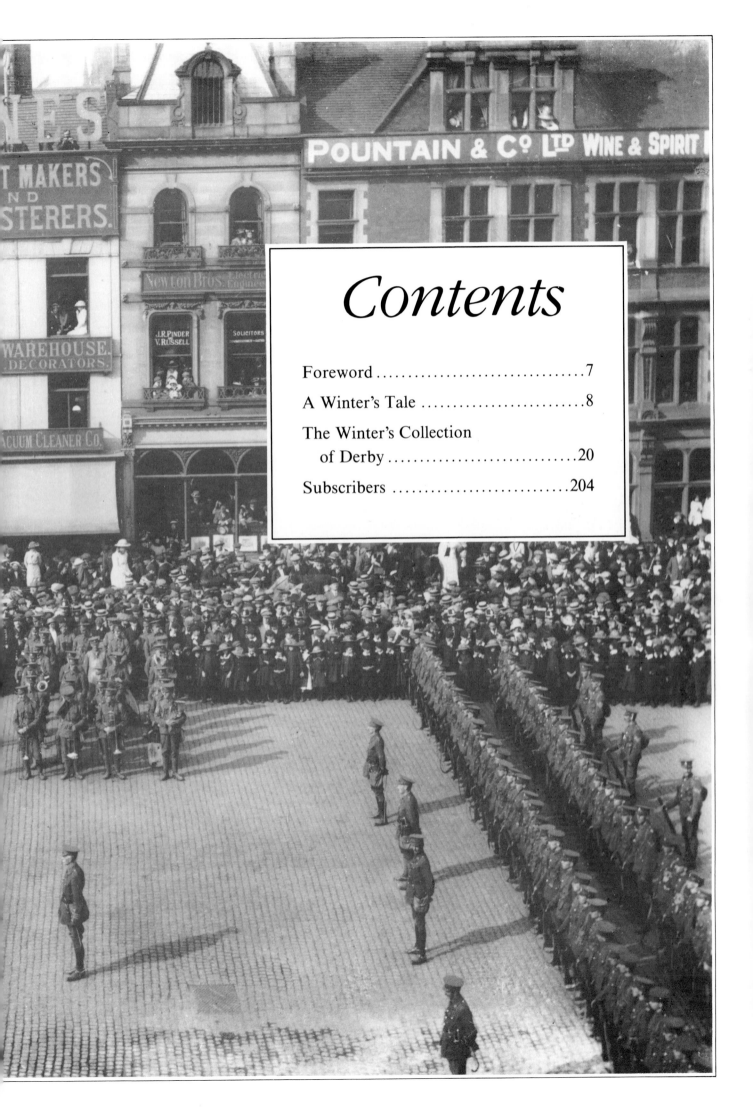

Contents

This book is dedicated

to the memory of

Charles Henry Barson

All the photographs featured in this book
are exclusively available for purchase from
W.W.Winter Ltd, Midland Road, Derby.
Tel: 0332 45224.

Foreword

SINCE the company's foundation in 1981, Breedon Books Publishing has been pleased to produce a number of high quality books on the history of Derby. Interest in the city's history has never been higher and it has been gratifying to receive so many kind remarks about Breedon's contribution to the published works on the subject.

Inevitably, photographs from the Winter Collection have formed the basis for many of the illustrated sections in these books and, indeed, most of the more famous views of old Derby have been taken by Winter's.

It is particularly pleasing for Breedon, then, to be able to publish this book based solely on Winter's work. A much wider range of photographs can be used, most of them unpublished until now.

It is particularly fitting that the book coincides with the 125th anniversary of Winter's removal to their present site in Midland Road. The book marks that anniversary and is a tribute to the huge contribution that the W.W. Winter business has made to Derby's rich and varied story.

Anton Rippon
Chairman,
The Breedon Books Publishing Company.

A Winter's Tale

by Angela Leeson

THE PHOTOGRAPHS in this book originate from the archives of just one Derby photographer — W.W.Winter Ltd. The Winter Collection, as the negatives are collectively named, represents a unique record of people, places and events relating to Derby since 'Winters' was established in 1867.

These glass negatives are a rich source of local history, especially as the majority have never before been published. The fact that many have been hand-printed from the original glass plates means that they are prints of the highest quality and it is somehow fitting that their first publication should occur in the year of W.W.Winter's 125th Anniversary.

William Walter Winter, the son of a Norfolk artist and the man whose name was to become synonymous with photography in Derby.

W.H.Fox-Talbot is credited with being the 'Father' of photography. It was in 1834 that the first photograph was taken by Fox-Talbot at Lacock Abbey. As far as Derby is concerned, it is believed that the Revd Edward Abney took the first photograph of the town and it was his son, Captain (later Sir William) Abney, who was the first president of the Derby Photographic Society when it was founded in 1884.

Of the many studios established in Derby in the early years, only W.W.Winter has survived. William Walter Winter was born in Great Yarmouth in May 1842, the son of a Norfolk artist. It was his father who first introduced him to photography. After an education at the Redenhall Academy, he arrived in Derby in about 1862.

In or before 1857, Monsieur Emmanuel Nicholas Charles founded a photographic business on Midland Road, but on the opposite side to the present-day premises.

When Winter arrived in Derby, he found employment fairly quickly, as an assistant to Charles. In 1864, Charles died, leaving his widow, Sarah, to carry on the business. She subsequently married Winter.

In 1867, Winter relocated the business on the other side of Midland Road,

The original 'Winter's' shop and studio on Midland Road, opposite today's premises. This photograph must have been taken between 1864, when Winter took over the business from Nicholas Charles, and 1867, when the present purpose-built photographic studio was built.

Winter's studio, now called the Alexandra Rooms and proudly boasting the business's royal connections with King Edward VII and the Princess of Wales.

Interior of the studio, showing a young Winter standing by the camera.

in a new purpose-built photographic studio, and re-named it after himself. These are the same premises that are used today. It was built with a row of large windows which were needed to provide the studio with natural daylight and were north-facing to protect it from direct sunlight. At the time this was the only form of light available for studio photography.

Winter himself became an institution in the town, treating photography as more than just a trade. He had a well-earned reputation and, whereas the other main Derby photographer, Richard Keene, specialised in landscape and architecture, Winter specialised in portraiture.

His portraits, described as having an 'exquisite softness, delicacy and beauty', were exhibited all around the world, winning many medals. For example, a gold medal was won in Caernarfon in 1886, another gold was won in India in 1889, and a silver medal was won in Philadelphia in 1893 to name but a few.

However, it was a photograph of an old, blind beggar which won possibly the widest acclaim. The original photograph, which featured the beggar, Mr John Darwin with a local girl called Ethel Ward, is still on display at 'Winters' today.

Winter was a member of the Derby Photographic Society from its first year up to 1909. He was also very active in local politics as a Conservative town councillor and his portraits of successive Mayors of Derby adorned the walls of the Town Hall.

In the mid 1880s, there was a disastrous fire at the Midland Road studio and Winter took the opportunity to remodel the building and, at the same time, enlarge it considerably.

He added another studio for portraiture, an artists' room, retouching room and so on. Behind the shop front were some thirty rooms in total. Several

The photograph which won the Winter's business most acclaim. Blind beggar Mr John Darwin pictured with a local girl named
Ethel Ward.

Views of the galleries at Winter's, 'the largest and most complete in character in the United Kingdom'.

William Henry King, who joined the business as a photographic assistant in 1896, for a wage of £2 per week. In 1910 he and Henry Bernard Sheppard bought out W.W.Winter and in 1930 King acquired sole ownership. Winter's is still run by his family today.

of these were used as galleries, where photographs, paintings and other *objets d'art* were exhibited. At the time those galleries were pronounced 'the largest and most complete of their character in the United Kingdom'.

On 21 November 1896, William Henry King joined the business as a photographic assistant, operator and retoucher. His initial wage was just two pounds per week. At the time he had to sign an agreement never to set up his own photographic business within a twenty-mile radius of Derby.

Mention has already been made about the forced reliance upon natural daylight in photography and, also, in printing and in retouching. So much depended on the weather and the length of daytime that the development of artificial lighting became imperative.

Winter was also one of the pioneers in the use of flash-light photography. On 19 March 1900, he gave a lecture at the Municipal Technical College on 'Portraiture by Flashlight' and amazed his audience when his assistant, W.H.King, took a photograph using flash powder. Winter must also be considered a pioneer in the use of electric lighting.

In fact, the flexibility which both forms of artificial lighting introduced

Above: Photographic assistants printing by daylight on the roof of Winter's premises. This inflexible method required much skill and judgement as the intensity of the light could not be controlled. On a bright day, prints could be exposed in minutes, whereas on dull days it might take hours.

Left: This very rare photograph shows the studio and the then modern carbon-arc equipment. Made by Davis of Derby, this piece of equipment was one of the very first forms of electric photographic lighting. The electricity was produced by a small generator situated in the stables at the rear of the premises.

into photography was revolutionary. For example, as one of Winter's advertisements stated: "Even on dull or foggy days, Mr Winter's Portraits are taken by the aid of Electric Light."

On 13 July 1904, W.H.King was promoted to the post of 'Head Operator and General Manager' for the wage of three pounds and ten shillings per week.

Meanwhile, Winter's reputation spread. He was patronised by many dignitories, including the Duke and Duchess of Devonshire, Major General Baden-Powell, and he was by Royal Appointment to HM King Edward VII.

Sometimes Winter used to photograph the King and other members of the Royal Family when they were staying at either Chatsworth or Rangemoor. One of Winter's portrait studies of the King was hung in the Derby Art Gallery Exhibition in 1906.

On one occasion, he was asked to photograph the King at Chatsworth on a Sunday. Being a highly religious man, he asked if another day could be chosen as he did not want to ask his operators to work on a Sunday. The Royal Party, apparently, were sympathetic and another day was chosen.

On 12 August 1910, W.H.King and Henry Bernard Sheppard formed a partnership and bought the business from Winter for the sum of £2,000. Winter subsequently emigrated to Canada where he married twice more and was ordained as a Minister of the Church. He died in February 1925.

In 1930, Sheppard sold his interest in the company to W.H.King, whose family have owned it ever since.

It was World War Two which inadvertently brought about the next significant change in the company. Because, like most other things, photographic materials were rationed and members of staff were away, either fighting or working elsewhere for the war effort, the business became greatly reduced in size.

Photograph of Winter's staff with W.H.King second from the left of the back row and H.B.Sheppard in the middle.

This photograph shows a young Hubert, aged 14, with his Uncle Austin, learning about daylight printing. The other figure is technician Edna Longford.

Charles Barson, who made an invaluable contribution to the formation of the Winter's Collection.

This portrait of Hubert
King, the current
managing director, was
taken in the studio at
W.W.Winter.

W.H.King's youngest son, Austin, who was by then the main portrait
photographer, was himself absent for much of the time during the war, serving
as a special constable. It was largely due to this staff shortage that King's
grandson, Hubert (by his other son, Howard), was called upon to help out.
This was the start of his lifelong association with the company.

After the war and until he retired in 1947, W.H.King was able to pass
on much of his knowledge and experience, accumulated since the 1890s, to
his grandson. Hubert was very fortunate that this learning process was continued
by his Uncle Austin, who subsequently became the managing director. Hubert
learnt at first hand every aspect of photography, printing and retouching.

This background, combined with a four-year City and Guilds course at
Nottingham College of Arts and Crafts, means that Hubert has been the most
comprehensively-trained photographer that the company has ever had. He
became the managing director in August 1975 and is continuing the tradition

This photograph shows Joseph Stack, the photographic manager of W.W.Winter, and Angela Leeson, the company's general manager, looking at a 15in x 12in glass negative taken from the Winter's Collection. These negatives are difficult to print, each one presenting its own particular problems in relation to its size, condition and density. It is Joe who has printed the majority of the photographs in this book, using skills which in general are rarely used in photographic practice today.

of passing on to the next generation, the skills and knowledge which were passed down to him.

No historical account of W.W.Winter would be complete without a brief mention of Charles Henry Barson. 'Charlie' started work for the company in 1928. He was employed as both a photographer and printer until his retirement in June 1981.

However, his association with 'Winters' did not end there. He usually spent one day a week at the studio sorting through the old negative files, right up until his death in December 1989. His knowledge and memories were crucial in the identification of many of the negatives. It is his contribution which has, without doubt, made the formation of the Winter Collection possible.

W.W.Winter's long history is a tribute to its continuing high standards. Still involved in both social and commercial photography, the business of today is a unique mix of the old and the new. It has had to change with the times, successfully adopting the innovations of the twentieth century whilst not forgetting many of the traditional methods. For example, the skills of hand printing, sepia toning and retouching are still as valuable today as they were a hundred years go.

Indeed, the business seems to have come full circle. Recently, 'Winters' has seen a large increase in demand for the copying and restoration of old photographs. Some of those brought in for this service were actually taken by 'Winters' many years ago! It is always very pleasing to see them and to feel that the people of Derby have the same confidence in W.W.Winter today as their ancestors did before them.

We hope that you will enjoy this look at just a part of the Winter Collection.

Derby Market Place as it should be, with market stalls. This photograph is dated about 1900. The Assembly Rooms are at the left of the picture with Ramsden's Restaurant next door. The building next to the latter is Edgar Horne's music shop. Note the lead-roofed cabbies rest in front of the Guildhall and attractive triple of lamp standards.

The Market Place from Irongate, c.1908.

The statue of Michael Thomas Bass MP (died 1884) by Sir John Boehm, Bt, 1885, in its original position on the west side of the Market Place, c.1890. The statue is now in Museum Square.

The north and east sides of the Market Place, seen from the Cornmarket around 1910. Note the Cabbies' Rest and Hansom cabs awaiting hire. Bass's statue of 1885 stands to the left. 'P. Wood/Seedsman' marks Newcastle House, an Elizabethan structure rebuilt around 1680 and destroyed in 1971.

Market Place, east side with War Memorial, around 1925.

The Market Place in 1924 with the War Memorial newly-completed. It was designed by C.A.Thompson and the sculpture was by
A.G.Walker ARA, both local men. The memorial was unveiled on 11 November 1924 by Alderman Oswald Ling, who as Mayor
in 1922, had inaugurated the project.

The grimy but seemly Palladian façade of the Assembly Rooms at the corner of the Market Place and Full Street, photographed *c.*1931. Designed by Washington Shirley, 5th Earl Ferrers, built by Joseph Pickford, 1773-43, Tympannium carved by Ratcliffe of Nottingham. A corner of Erasmus Darwin's house at 3 Full Street is visible extreme left.

Market Place, 30 October 1931. A famous photograph of the Assembly Rooms with Ramsden's Restaurant beside it. Exactly 200 years later, the building suffered minor damage in a fire and was quickly demolished, except for the façade, which is now at the Crich Tramway Museum.

Ramsden's Restaurant, next to the Assembly Rooms. Built in 1765 at the expense of Brian Hodgson, landlord of the Old Hall Hotel, Buxton, by Joseph Pickford, it was to supply suppers to the Assemblies. The Ramsden's firm was founded in 1886 and was moved to the Market Place *c.*1909 by Horace Ramsden, then to the Cornmarket (where it later became a Berni Inn) in 1946.

The elegant interior of the Assembly Rooms *c.*1931. The interior decoration was designed by no less a person than Robert Adam and executed by Pickford's *stuccadore* Abraham Denstone (d.1779) in 1774. A small fire at the far end in February 1963 gave the then Borough Council the excuse to demolish the entire building. The girandoles are now in Pickford's House Museum and a chandelier survives in the Mayor's Reception Suite at the Council House.

Market Place, view towards Market Head *c.*1934. The market stalls were banished, rather short-sightedly perhaps — a year or two earlier, to be replaced by motor-cars.

Right: Guildhall (Henry Duesbury, 1842), photographed *c.*1935. Opposite page: The Guildhall lit overall during the celebrations for the Centenary of the Municipal Corporations Act 1835, in September 1935. Opportunity was also taken to mark the Silver Jubilee of King George V. An exhibition of municipal achievements was also held.

A full meeting of Derby Borough Council at the Guildhall is posed for the camera between the wars. Council meetings were moved to the Council House around 1948. Photographs of former Mayors of Derby can be seen behind. They were taken by W.W.Winter.

Strutt's Calico Mill which stood on what is now Osnabrück Square. Built for Jedediah Strutt by his son William Strutt FRS (1756-1830) as a 'fire-proof' mill, it was damaged by fire in 1852 and in 1876 (not long after the date of this fascinating photograph), when it was pulled down. It was the tallest secular building in Derby.

Market Place, south side and Guildhall c.1950. To the right of the Guildhall, the *Derbyshire Advertiser* office, converted from the Regency bow-fronted Cross Keys inn, with Frost's butcher's shop beyond.

Albert Street looking towards the Corn Exchange (Benjamin Lisbon, 1861) which was sold to the *Derby Daily Telegraph* as works and offices in 1928. On left, the Albert Street 'Bus Station. Photograph of *c.*1930.

Morledge: looking NW with empty market stalls, Brookhouse's Roman Cement Works and the Shot Tower, *c.*1931.

Albert Street from Tenant Bridge c.1938. Note the Exchange Hotel (1863) and Corn Exchange, which dominates the view. All in this view survive except the Co-op store (R.Bridgart, 1865) at right.

Morledge: Cox's Lead Works, showing the Shot Tower, erected in 1809 and demolished in 1932. Some demolition has already taken place at the base, so the date must be around that time. View taken from the east, looking towards the Guildhall (tower, right).

Morledge from Cockpit Hill, Bus Station on right. On left the White Horse Inn. Photograph of c.1936.

Cattle Market Bridge, 30 October 1931, looking towards Cockpit Hill. All this was swept away in 1968 to make way for the Inner Ring Road.

Cockpit Hill: The new 'Bus Station under construction, 1932, being Phase One of the Derby Central Improvement Scheme. The contractors were Gee, Walker & Slater of Uttoxeter Old Road.

Cattle Market Bridge showing Lodge at the corner of Cattle Market, looking NW. Note the dome of the Corn Market in the distance (left). Designed by George Thompson and H.I.Stevens, 1861. Demolished 1967.

Cockpit Hill: the same view as the preceding taken after completion in May 1933, with the Open Market (opened June 1932) beyond. Right background are the Derwent Flats, Exeter Place, built 1931 under the provisions of the 1930 Housing Act.

Cockpit Hill: The newly-completed 'Bus Station, looking ESE. The design (by C.H.Aslin and H.V.Lem Chester) was innovative, being based on railway practice. The currature of the platforms was dictated by the restricted site. The Art-Deco building, left, is the Markets Office. Note the Cattle Market beyond (Stevens and Thompson, 1861).

Moriedge: Riverside Gardens, the grand canal, with its bronze turtles, looking NW from the River Derwent towards Tenant Street. Note the rear of the Open Market, left. The Council House is yet to be started, so the date is probably 1934-35. The Gardens have since been cut back (for the Crown Court) and the turtles are now at Allestree Hall. This illustration appears in the 1935 *Borough Directory*.

Cockpit Hill: Bus Station, newly completed, spring 1933. Most of Aslin's buildings were basically classical, but here all was Art-Deco modernism, but in local brick with good quality detailing. Note the Daimler limousine, right: the owner of such a car could surely not have needed to catch a bus?

Riverside Gardens: newly completed 1934. The Council House site has been cleared, but work had to be postponed due to financial restrictions and did not start until 1938. The arch (centre) was built to allow the Markeaton Brook to enter the Derwent. Note the fine bronze lamps with thistle finials. This illustration also appears in the 1935 *Borough Directory*.

Derwent Street East, south side, looking from Phoenix Street down Exeter Street. At right, the Congregational Chapel with the White Lion Inn on the corner. The imposing terrace of Regency houses in Exeter Street included No 12, where on 27 July 1820 the great Victorian philosopher Herbert Spencer (d.1903) was born, Photograph of *c*.1920, when the area had become rather run down. All demolished 1960.

Derwent Street, pictured in October 1931 with Harwood's printing works and the Market Tavern, closed prior to demolition to make way for the Council House.

Derwent Street. View east on 30 October 1931. In the distance, the Royal Standard Inn of c.1895 (still extant) and the old printing works, demolished in 1940.

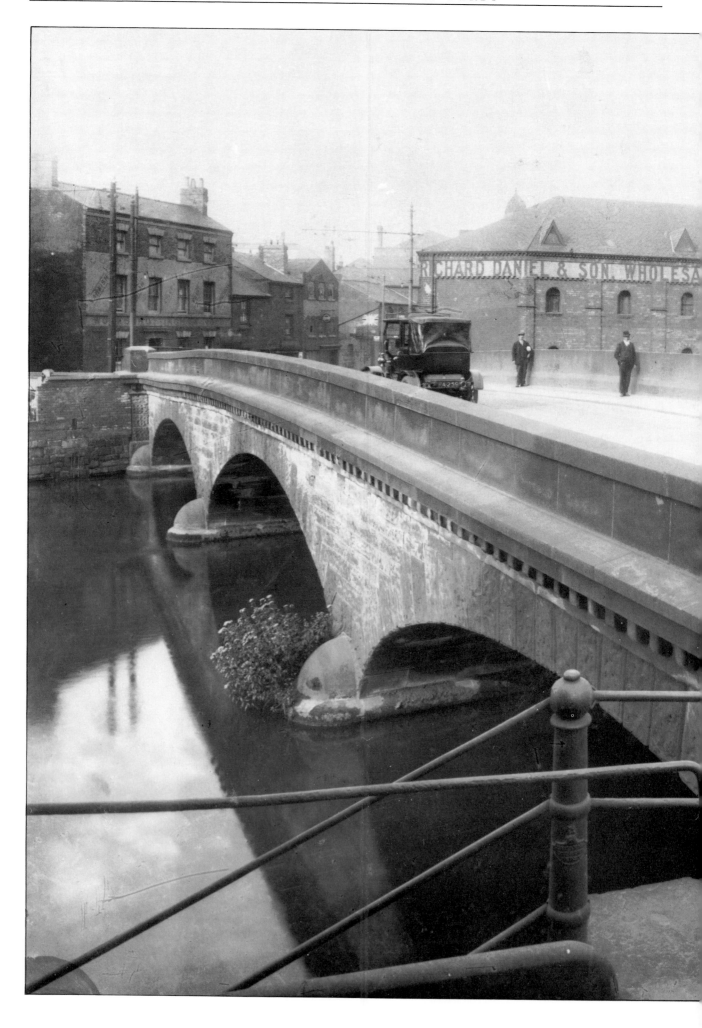

Derwent Street, Exeter Bridge, before it was replaced in 1931. It was built in 1850 to the designs of Richard Trubshaw. The buildings to the right were demolished in 1931 to make way for the Central Improvement Scheme. Beyond Richard Daniel's warehouse, Burleigh Street.

Derwent Street: Old Exeter Bridge seen in the late 1920s.

St Mary's Bridge Chapel and House, *c.*1922. The 15th-century chapel (of 13th-century origin) stood on the bridge's predecessor, demolished in 1792 when Thomas Harrison of Chester finished the present one. It was purchased by the Derbyshire Archaeological Society 1928 and restored 1930. The house (behind the chapel) dated 1700, for a long time the home of the Eaton family, was rebuilt 1790 by John and Charles Finney.

River Derwent looking NW: Exeter Bridge from Cattle Market Bridge in the late 1920s. Left to right: gardens of houses in Tenant Street (later the site of the Council House), All Saints' tower, the Power Station with its taller 1926 extension behind and (just visible) the bell tower of the Silk Mill.

Derwent Street: the yard of G.S.Oscroft and Co, motor engineers. Their recovery vehicle has just brought in a failed 12hp Vauxhall . . .or has it all been staged for the camera? *c.*1938. The premises are today part of Kennings.

Full Street. Site of old swimming baths, then recently knocked down, 1933. An electricity cable is being paid out towards river. Note, in background the Gothick, stair window of P.P.Burdett's house, designed by Pickford for his friend, the cartographer, *c.*1765.

The old baths stood next to the Corporation Power Station and the cable presumably was planned to terminate in it. The remainder is here seen floating down the Derwent in a southerly direction. Note the Old Silk Mill in background.

Full Street: The Old Horse and Trumpet Inn in its late 17th-century gabled brick building, seen under ownership of Ludlam Ramsden, son of neighbouring restauranter H.E.Ramsden, *c.*1925. He sold to Offiler's brewery, who in 1928 pulled down this delightful old inn and replaced it with a banal affair in 'Stockbroker's Tudor'.

Derwent Street: G.F.Tomlinson & Sons begin work preparing the foundations of the new Council House, 1937. Behind is C.H.Aslin's Magistrates' Court building, then barely three years old.

Tenant Bridge, Tenant Street. Bank's chandlery shop, c.1875. The firm later moved to Brook Street.

Corporation Street: The Council House, newly completed c.1949, with the Magistrates' Court and Police Station beyond (1934), all by C.H.Aslin. Had the war not intervened, Aslin was planning to build an oval Council Chamber on the car-park (right). The war also led to a scaling down of detailing of the Council House, including the deletion of a stone clock-tower over the entrance facing Full Street.

Tenant Bridge, October 1931. Junction of Albert Street (left), Tenant Street (Centre) and Morledge (behind camera). The presence of the bridge is betrayed by the rise in the carriageway. Note the Thorntree Inn (built c.1785) left of centre, cleared shortly afterwards as part of the Central Improvement Scheme. In the distance is Pountain's, Market Place.

Tenant Bridge from the north, 30 October 1931. Note the base of the Shot Tower and surviving parapet of the medieval Tenant Bridge (left) and Cockpit Hill in the distance.

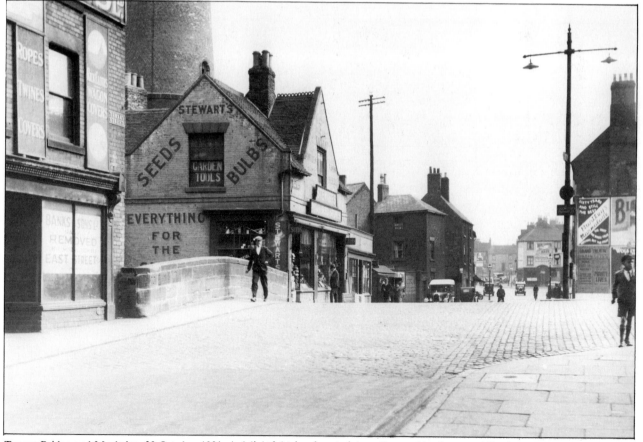

Tenant Bridge and Morledge, 30 October 1931. A delightful trio of post-vintage thoroughbred automobiles decorate the kerb.

Tenant Street, 30 October 1931, a street which today hardly exists. The building left is Morris House, previously Britannia House (Benjamin Wilson) demolished 1986; another vanished sight is the policeman on point duty. To the right is the Royal Oak Inn, rebuilt in 1890 and closed in 1916, after which it became offices.

Cornmarket, view to north with buildings and trams decorated to commemorate the Coronation of George V, 1911.

Cornmarket, looking north, c.1914. The St James' Hotel (Giles and Brookhouse, 1866) dominates the scene and its corner site has yet to be adapted as Barclay's Bank. The tram is serving route 12 — Uttoxeter Road (Constable's Lane)—Town Centre-Burton Road (Borough Boundary).

Cornmarket, looking north c.1935. Guy BTX trolleybus has just arrived from Allestree (right).

Cornmarket, looking north, from ground level, *c.*1928.

Cornmarket looking north from St Peter's Bridge, *c.*1925. In distance, Barlow, Taylor is being built. The photograph well emphasises the hump in the foreground caused by the presence of the bridge, still lurking beneath the road.

St James's Street, corner of Cornmarket. Two of the three exotic Victorian buildings of 1871 still stand. They show G.H.Sheffield in Gothic, Norman and Lombardic styles. Yeoman's tobacconist's eventually moved to the top of Sadler Gate and closed about 1979. A scene pictured in 1920.

Victoria Street, looking from outside the Post Office Hotel (now Lloyd's) towards Wardwick. Centre is the corner building of the Refuge Assurance by Giles and Brookhouse, 1870. Left of it is the Mechanics' Institute, by Arthur Coke Hill and G.H.Sheffield, 1882. Note the delightful cast-iron tram shelter. Photograph of c.1926.

Victoria Street with a single-decker Trent 'bus approaching, c.1936. Note Ranby's store, left, a collection of 18th-century buildings all run together and united with hoardings. All replaced by the present Debenhams in 1962.

Victoria Street, south side, showing Edward Johnson's, clockmakers. A notable firm, founded 1857, it closed on the death of Edward Johnston Jnr in 1932, when the buildings were demolished to make way for Burton's. Note Clulow's bookshop. Photograph of c.1885.

St James's Street, No 20. The jeweller's shop of Joseph V. Woodward, about 1925. Francis and Thomas Woodward had been apprentices of Whitehurst's, the latter being works manager there in 1851. Joseph, Francis' son, set up on Nottingham Road, and this shop is that of his son, carrying the Whitehurst tradition into the 20th century.

St Peter's Bridge, looking along Victoria Street *c.*1937. Note the Royal Hotel (Robert Wallace, 1839) and the Brookside Presbyterian Church (T.C.Hine, 1861) beyond.

Victoria Street, view SE *c.*1905. At left, John Ward's Tramways Office (1903-04) with 1888 horse omnibus No 5 outside. Note charabanc in centre distance, with electric tramcars Nos 2 and 19.

St James' Bridge, about 1900. Right: the Post Office (by J.Williams, 1867), and left the St James' Street/Strand corner (Giles and Brookhouse, 1870-71).

St James's Bridge, c.1900. Left: St James' Street with Pickford's Lock Up Yard building in background. Right: Post Office Hotel (previously the Spotted Horse, a name revived in the 1960s) by G.H.Sheffield, 1871. Now called Lloyd's. The view is dominated by the GPO of 1867, a most impressive Italian Palazzo style building. The medieval St James' Bridge is still buried beneath the surface of Victoria Street at this point.

Victoria Street, Coronation Buildings. The range which, in this 1930s view, contained Woolworth's (which moved to the Eagle Centre in 1976) was so called because it was built in 1911, the year of King George V's Coronation. The Derbyshire Building Society put their building up in 1878, but later moved to 7 Irongate.

Victoria Street: A similar view to the preceding, but photographed in the early 1950s, after the former Derbyshire Building Society had been shop-fronted.

The Strand Arcade from The Strand *c*.1900. Built to a design by John Story 1880-1881, it was a conscious imitation of London's Burlington Arcade.

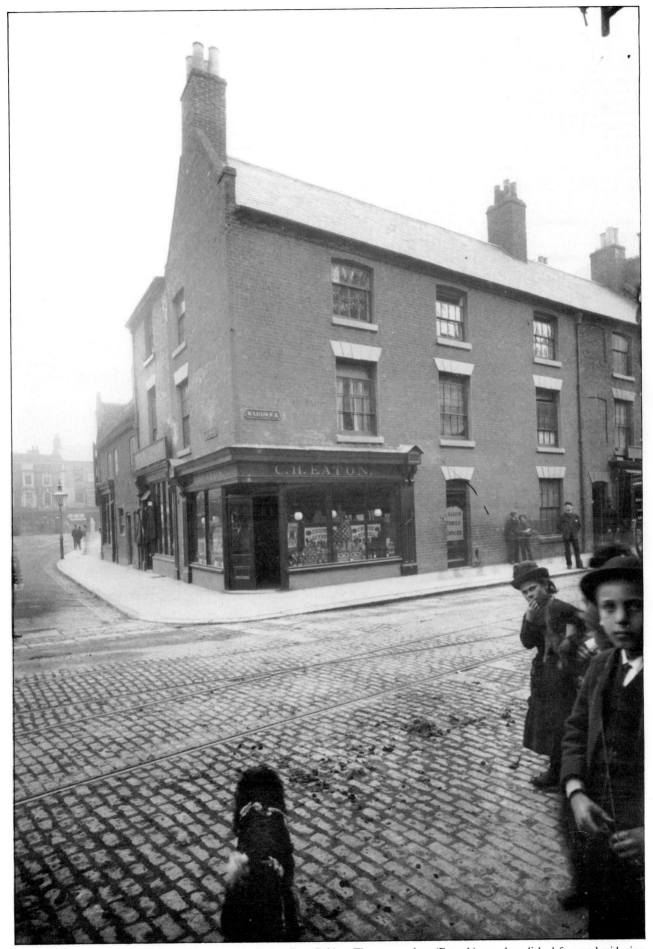

Wardwick: corner of Cheapside, looking towards Sadler Gate Bridge. The corner shop (Eaton's) was demolished for road widening in 1913. Photograph of *c.*1890.

Wardwick: The Jacobean House's garden, with the converted gothick stable block, to right, destroyed in 1969. Behind can be seen the tower of the Library and the roof of Mundy House. Photograph of *c*.1890, when Jacobean House was inhabited by a solicitor.

Jacobean House, Wardwick. The remaining garden, *c*.1890. The urn atop the hall was rescued from the 1731 Guildhall in 1828. Note the Poor Law Guardians' offices in Becket Street, beyond. Now Berlin's 'fun pub'.

Wardwick, looking west, c.1909. The fine railings in front of the Museum, by Alderman William Haslam, were mainly destroyed in 1942.

Wardwick: Derby Free Library and Museum (R.K.Freeman, 1879) with newly-completed extension of 1915 (centre, left) by T.H.Thorpe. Far left can be glimpsed the back of the Art Gallery (J.S.Story, 1882).

Wardwick, looking SE, about 1914. Derby Museum (left) with the Mechanics' Institute (A.Coke-Hill and G.H.Sheffield, 1882) beyond. The Jacobean House and Becket Street can be seen, right.

Wardwick, looking SE, about 1934. Derby Free Library and Museum (R.K.Freeman 1879) on left.

Sadler Gate, No 49. Thomas Frost's pork butcher's shop, *c.*1900. He also had a branch in the Market Place and another in Normanton Road at this time.

Although called the Chaddesden Milk Dairy, this shop is Holmes and Moore, Curzon Street, with a rebuilt shop front *c.*1893.

Curzon Street, No 56: Holmes and Moore's dairy and grocer's shop and corner of Friary Street, now a furnishing emporium, photographed in 1888.

Cheapside: Nos 7-8, Staton and Cooper's paint shop. Their works was on City Road, Little Chester. The business was taken over by Gurth Cooper alone by 1900. Photograph of c.1888.

Friar Gate: junction with Curzon Street (left) and Cheapside (right), showing the newly-rebuilt church of St Werburgh (Sir Arthur Blomfield, 1894-6). The vehicle in the foreground is a reminder that Cheapside then (c.1899) had a cab range. The Buck in the Park Inn (today rather heavily rebuilt) goes back to c.1820.

Cheapside (St Werburgh's Church Yard): a delightful view of c.1890. The church is seen as built in 1699, with classical dome-lit nave and tower of 1610. It was largely rebuilt four years later. Note the cabbies' rest and solitary 'growler'. The ends of side roads were cobbled across to ensure a dry passage for pedestrians in an era of muddy streets.

Friar Gate, looking west *c*.1927 with an LNER train crossing the ornate bridge made by Andrew Handyside and Co, 1876. The Ford Street/Stafford Street junction is in foreground. Note Alderman Cheshyre's House of 1708, right.

Friar Gate: The south front of the Friary in the Bodens' time c.1890. The central block was the original house of 1730; the wing to the right was added in 1760; that on the left c.1880, to house the ballroom. Subsequent extensions have wrecked this aspect of the house, which has been an hotel since c.1922.

Friar Gate: famous wartime view showing Handyside's bridge and lamp standards painted with blackout stripes. Note the 1938 Morris 8 at the kerb with the Corporation omnibus undertaking's tower-wagon behind.

Friar Gate: Royal School for the Deaf (R.Ernest Ryley, 1893-4) with the Great Northern Railway bridge. Photograph of c.1898.

Ashbourne Road: sandwiched between Ashbourne Road Council School (now Ashgate School) and the Methodist church was the works of Messrs Burrows and Sturgess, seen here c.1935 with delivery vehicle from an earlier age. Their factory, which made soft drinks, has long since been demolished.

South Street: Derby's County Gaol (1826 by Francis Goodwin) was largely demolished in 1928, leaving the façade gracing a greyhound track built on the site in 1930. In this view it was still under construction.

South Street: The newly-completed Greyhound Stadium lit up for an evening meeting *c.*1931.

East Street: Derby Co-operative Society's 1928 building, a handsome classical design on the corner of Albion Street by A.N.Bromley. Now punctured by a first-floor bridge and looking dowdy, it was new when this photograph was taken *c.*1928.

East Street (Bag Lane): umbrella emporium of Alderman Arthur Simpson (1851-1917), Mayor of Derby in 1907. The young proprietor is pictured at the door c.1882. He later served as president of the National Chamber of Commerce. His son was Sir George Simpson, FGS, the celebrated meteorologist.

St Peter's Street: junction with St Peter's Church Yard (left) and East Street (centre) before the building of Boots in 1890. In the centre is Sir Edwin Ann's Midland Drapery complex, founded 1882, the building going up in three phases (under three separate architects, the corner part being by G.H.Sheffield) 1887-1892.

St Peter's Street, Midland Drapery in the 1920s. The building has been colour-washed and the parapet fitted with the well-known magnet 'that draws the people'. Closed and demolished in 1970, it is now the site of the lacklustre Audley Centre. Note how the façade of the part in the left has been shorn of all ornament.

East Street: Midland Drapery second phase building of 1890-1891, photographed in the 1920s.

St Peter's Street. Midland Drapery leather goods department, *c.*1920s.

St Peter's Street from The Spot *c.*1935. Babington Lane joins at left. Note brand new MG parked on right. Today the driver would be given a parking-ticket very swiftly.

St Peter's St from The Spot. Babington Lane can be seen, left. The tall gabled building is Babington Buildings of 1898, which replaced demolished Babington House. Photograph taken c.1908.

St Peter's Street looking north, 1923. One of the trams still has not received its top cover even at this late date. Note the White Hall Cinema (right) which opened 1913 (designed by T.H.Thorpe) and became the Odeon in 1935, closing in 1965.

St Peter's Street from The Spot, with Babington Lane, left. A Guy BTX trolley bus (No 44 of 1932) approaches the camera, c.1935.

St Peter's Street: interior and procenium arch of the Odeon, photographed when newly-rebuilt in 1935. It opened as the White Hall Cinema.

St Peter's Street: ground-floor showroom of the Central Educational Ltd, photographed *c.*1938.

St Peter's Street: interior of the showrooms of the Central Educational, showing the well-stocked book department *c.*1938.

St Peter's Street: from Babington Buildings about 1898. Holbrook House is the tall building (centre). At left, G.S.Smith, one of the sons of clockmaker John Smith of Queen Street, who broke away and started his own rival firm.

St Peter's Street: corner of Thorntree Lane. The corner building was built for the Prudential Assurance Company around the period of World War One. Yet within 20 years, it and the 18th-century building next door were demolished to make way for a new Marks and Spencer's.

St Peter's Street. corner of Thorntree Lane: the same site as the previous view, about 18 years later. Marks and Spencer's has recently opened. The pay-off with the Prudential was that they were allowed offices above. The Irish Linen Company are having a sale.

St Peter's Street, strangely deserted, shortly after the opening of Marks and Spencer (left) in the mid-1930s.

St Peter's Street, No 59 (Victoria House), the furnishing shop of Henry Shackleton, shown standing outside, in the 1890s. The pretty building of 1878 (when Shackleton's previous shop at the corner of St Peter's Church Yard was demolished) was taken over by the Midland Drapery (next door, right) around 1902, when the firm moved to the Wardwick. C.J.Shackleton, later a memorable Serjeant-at-Mace, was Henry's brother.

St Peter's Church Yard, looking east, c.1919. 'Marrowbones' chapel of 1826 was built by three butchers (hence the name) for their congregation. Boots, on St Peter's Street (corner of East Street) in the distance, was built in 1912 to a design by Albert Nelson Bromley of Nottingham, with statues of four local worthies by Morley Harder.

St Peter's Church Yard: YMCA building, the Victoria Hall of 1889, pictured in the early part of the present century. Rowell's and Winters occupied the shop units for the first three decades of the century, so precise dating is difficult.

Queen Street showing the street as widened in 1873, with the Corporation fire tender, the celebrated 'Niagara', against the kerbs. 'Niagara' was pensioned-off in 1888, eight years after the tramlines were laid down this street.

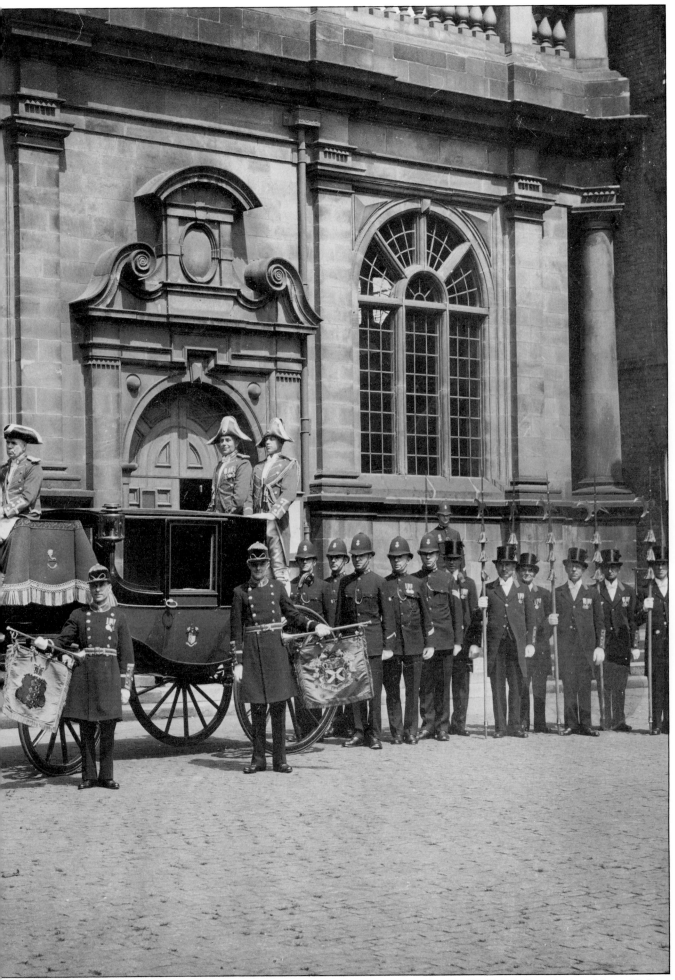

Installation of the High Sheriff at the Shire Hall, St Mary's Gate, in 1934. The High Sheriff, Sir Iain Peter Andrew Monro Walker, 3rd Bt (1902-1982), is accompanied by two trumpeters with banners of his and the Sovereign's arms, pikemen and halberdiers. He lived at Osmaston Hall, Ashbourne, and in 1956 succeeded to the Okeover estates, adding their name to his.

Queen Street, view south, c.1921. Note how the tower of All Saints' church dominates. In the 18th century, a man slid, with a donkey, on a rope from the top to a spot close to that occupied by the photographer.

Queen Street, looking north. All Saints' church looms on the right, with, beyond, the Dolphin, the Bull's Head, St Michael's and St Alkmund's. The buildings in the left, at the top of St Mary's Gate, were built (by Naylor and Sale) in 1923. However, Queen Street Baths have yet to be built, so the photograph is of c.1926.

Walker Lane (Cathedral Road): an impressive line-up of Mark 1 Land Rovers outside Kennings around 1948. Their classical showrooms (background, on the corner of Queen Street) are now a restaurant.

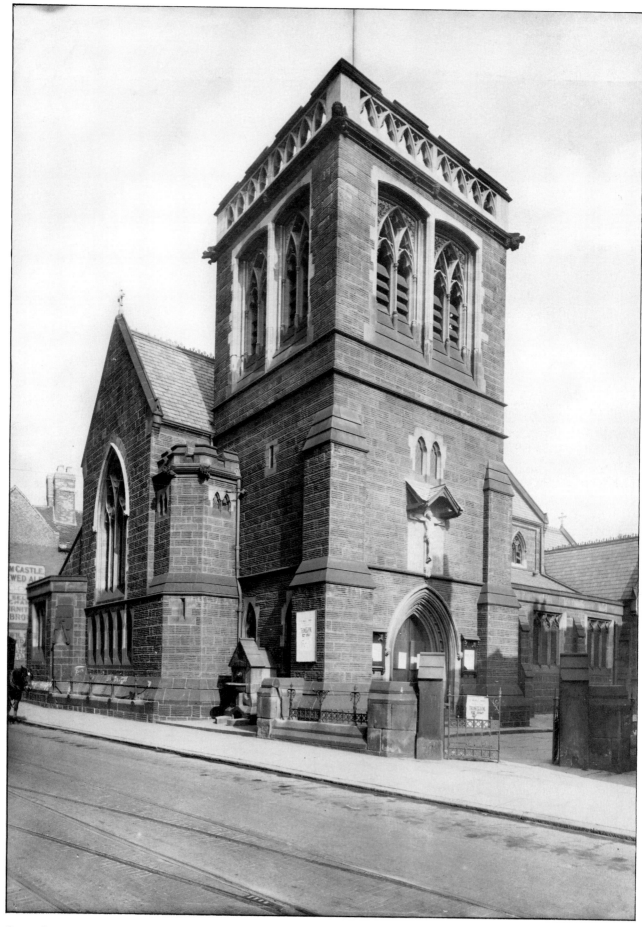

Queen Street: St Michael's Church, erected 1857 by H.I.Stevens to replace its medieval predecessor, which suffered a collapse the year before. Note the World War One war memorial over the entrance, dating the view to the period 1919-1930. Behind (right) is Alderman Haden's town-house; extreme left: Nottingham Castle Inn, corner of St Michael's Lane. The road is paved with wooden selts, an effort to reduce the noise of traffic in horse-drawn days.

Irongate, view north from Market Head *c.*1921. Tramcar No 27 was built in 1908 and given a top cover in 1913-14.

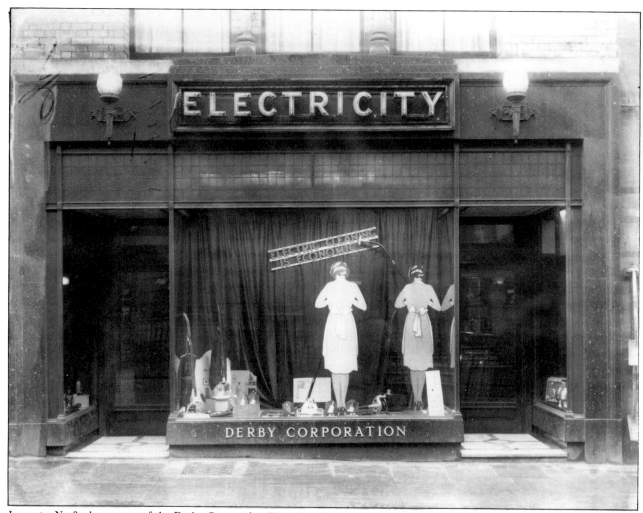

Irongate, No 9: showrooms of the Derby Corporation Electricity Department, *c*.1935. Note the marble-enriched Art-Deco Shopfront with its electric flambeaux over the doors, now all swept away.

King Street, Nos 3-5: Samuel Roome's fishmongery in the 1920s. The late 19th-century building was replaced by the one lately occupied by Eastern Treasures in 1969, when Roome's transferred to Sadler Gate, where they still flourish.

St Mary's Roman Catholic Church (A.W.N.Pugin and E.W.Pugin 1838-1844) viewed from St Alkmund's Church Yard, Derby's only Georgian Square. The fenestration of the Golden Lion Inn, corner of Bridge Gate, suggests a gabled building of 17th-century date, rebuilt in the later 18th century.

Bridge Gate: a delightful view of around 1925, looking towards St Alkmund's Church (H.I.Stevens, 1841-3, demolished 1967) and St Mary's Catholic Church. Centre, to the right of the lorry are the Wilmot Almshouses (founded 1634, rebuilt 1819). Centre right is the Nottingham Arms inn, a very ancient watering hole in a building with Derby windows of *c*.1795. The whole street was demolished in 1966.

North Street: Children's Hospital, designed in 1883 by Alexander MacPherson and seen here shortly after completion. Since vastly expanded but in 1992 under threat of closure.

Green Lane, looking towards Victoria Street, where part of the Athaneum Club can be seen. The low row of late 17th-century cottages still survive, but the remainder, including the (Bunch of) Grapes Tavern, nearest the camera, have gone. Photograph of c.1920.

Green Lane, looking south, *c*.1925. The vernacular cottages, left, survive, but the tall building beside them, and the Grapes Inn, failed to survive the 1960s. The building of Ramby's (Debenhams) in 1962 also accounted for the buildings on the right.

Babington Lane, The Grand Theatre (by Oliver Essex for A.Melville, 1886). It was the leading venue for music-hall and vandeville until competition arrived in the shape of the Hipprodome, Green Lane, in 1913. This view was taken *c.*1930. Note the commissionaire's proprietorial stance.

Babington Lane, looking east. The tramlines are still uncovered, yet trolley wires suggest the trams have finished, so the date is probably summer 1933. The St Peter's Street building marked 'Clothiers' is Mr Holbrook's town-house of 1828.

Babington Lane, just above Gower Street. The tramcar suggests a date of *c*.1932, but note the motor-bus, right, Grand Theatre, also right, and Joseph Wright School (Giles and Brookhouse, 1864) left, by the tramcar.

Babington Lane: Babington Buildings after the Public Benefit Boot and Shoe Company had revamped their display window in Art-Deco style *c*.1934, although the photograph could be from a few years after that date.

Babington Lane: Babington Buildings (1898), built by Councillor G.E.Franklin, founder of the Public Benefit Boot Company (in Hull, before he came to Derby). Photographed c.1933.

Ratcliffe's Toy Shop window on The Spot, lit up late one winter's afternoon in the late 1930s.

London Road, west side: Gaumont Palace Cinema, newly-built, 1934. Note that the tramlines have but recently been tarmacked over. Almost a classical design, but with rich Art-Deco detailing. Renamed the Odeon in 1965 and the New Trocadero in 1983.

London Road: interior of the Gaumont Palace Cinema, complete with Compton Organ and safety curtain. The Art-Deco interior is a tour-de-force. The organ was sold to St Philip's Catholic Church, Chaddesden, around 1965.

London Road: Derbyshire General Infirmary (Samuel Brown and William Strutt, 1806-1810) as rebuilt by H.I.Stevens in 1865. Demolished in 1892. The statue of Aesculapius on top was by the china modeller, William John Coffee, in terracotta.

London Road: the Derbyshire Royal Infirmary, newly built to the designs of Young and Hall, c.1898.

London Road: the Derbyshire Royal Infirmary Nurses' Home (Young & Hall, 1902) from the SE when new.

Probably a Hospital Day outfit, or perhaps a local eccentric?

Hospital Day c.1935. Once a year, in June, the Borough became *en fête* to raise money for the local hospitals. A procession wound through the town to Markeaton Park, consisting of numerous floats. This is Trent Motor Traction's contribution, c.1935. The junketings ended with the coming of the National Health Service in 1948.

London Road, looking NW from the tower of Holy Trinity church, c.1935. H.I.Stevens Congregational Chapel of 1846 (centre) is very prominent. It had been converted into a cinema in 1934.

London Road: a once well-known landmark, Bradley's Corner, on the junction with Burrough's Walk. Bradley's Ltd were well-known outfitters. The site was destroyed to build the Main Centre in the early 1960s. Photograph *c*.1937.

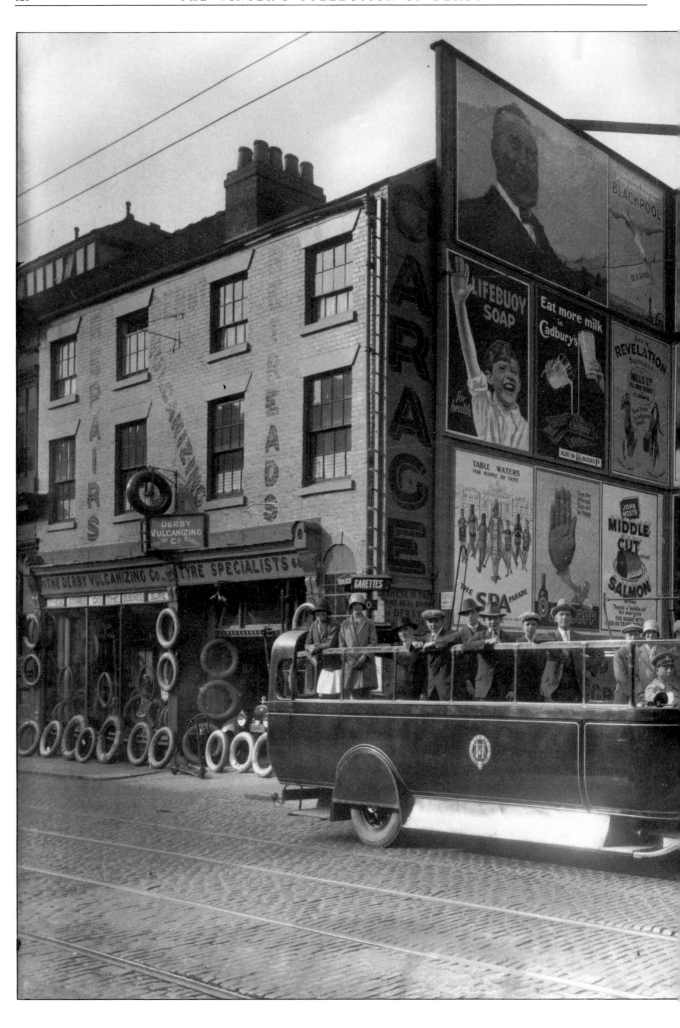

London Road, Nos 68-70: premises of the Derby Vulcanizing Company, tyre factors. The Trent charabanc appears to be part of a promotional wheeze, *c.*1928.

Traffic Street: grocery shop of John Taylor at No 28, *c*.1880. It was all swept away *c*.1931 when the street was slewed to the NE and drastically widened.

London Road (corner Traffic Street): Congregational Chapel by H.I.Stevens (1846-1848), a splendid classical essay with a giant Corninthian order converted into a cinema by T.H.Thorpe, 1934 and demolished for road widening in 1962. Note the Stag Inn, formerly the Stag and Thorn, Traffic Street (right). Some figures have been removed during the printing of this 1880s view.

London Road: a view of *c*.1907, showing what an elegant, tree-lined boulevard the street was. Partico of the Congregational Chapel (left) with Holy Trinity (1904) beyond and the Derbyshire Royal Infirmary to the right.

London Road: Methodist Chapel (Giles and Brookhouse 1861) on the corner of Canal Street. About 1919 it was rebuilt (as here, not long afterwards) and renamed Queen's Hall. Beresford's marble works, next door, was acquired and Queen's Hall Chambers built about the same time.

London Road: tram No 23 of 1904 pauses outside the Congregational Chapel *c.*1905. The large building, right, is Bradley's Corner; the railings are in front of the New Jerusalem Chapel of 1819.

London Road in the summer of 1914, looking north. Right: the Wesley and Methodist Chapel (now the Queen's Hall) and Cosy Cinema of 1913;, left: a corner of the Nottingham Arms Inn (now the Florence Nightingale) and, across Litchurch Street, the Leviathan Inn, newly rebuilt, but which was bought up and closed by the Derbyshire Royal Infirmary just before World War Two.

London Road, thanks to planting c.1873, a delightful tree-lined boulevard, seen here c.1909. The gates of the Derbyshire Royal Infirmary can be seen right. The church, left, is Holy Trinity, London Road, rebuilt 1904.

London Road, looking north *c*.1913. In the distance, Holy Trinity Church (1826, rebuilt 1904); to the right, Wesleyan Methodist Chapel (Giles and Brookhouse, 1861, now Queen's Hall); and the newly-opened Cosy Cinema, of which much of the interior survives as a restaurant.

Lake in Alvaston Park pictured in the 1920s. The park, of 30 acres, was established in 1913 and landscaped by William Barron's Ltd; the lake was added a decade later. Two young girls pose with a scooter and a small quadruped, probably called 'Patch'!

No 35 Horton Street was the shop of Alf Robey, wholesale greengrocer, who lived at 77 High Street. This is his lorry, posed outside Derby Wholesale Market *c*.1936.

Osmaston Road, view north of around 1935. The elegant Regency houses (right) have since been sacrificed to the growth of the Derbyshire Royal Infirmary.

Osmaston Road, looking north, *c.*1908 with the Baptist Church (T.C.Hine, 1862) in the distance. All the elegant villas on the right were demolished fairly recently to allow for the enormous expansion of the Derbyshire Royal Infirmary .

Osmaston Road c.1906. At right is T.C.Hine's Baptist Church of 1862 (demolished and replaced in 1970). It was largely paid for by Alderman Robert Pegg, Mayor in 1855, and whose exotically gothic house (also by Hine, and which survives) can be seen between the church and the tram.

Midland Road on 15 July 1881, decorated for the visit of HRH Prince and Princess of Wales, who came to open the Royal Agricultural Show on Osmaston Park. The building at left is Winter's Studio (The Alexandra Rooms) built by W.W.Winter's friend, Henry Isaac Stevens in 1867 and still in use by the firm today.

Midland Road, view from London Road towards the Railway Station c.1909. On the left is the Crown and Cushion of 1853; on the right, an elegant early Victorian building demolished in 1912 to make way for the present NatWest Bank.

Midland Road (originally Station Street) looking from London Road towards the Railway Station, c.1925. A fine Lancia rests at the kerb beside W.W.Winter's premises.

Midland Road, c.1914, the same view as the preceding but after the replacement of the corner building (right) with the present bank.

Midland Road, looking towards London Road on 13 November 1888, with triumphal arch to welcome the visit of Edward, Prince of Wales. Since the 1881 visit, the elegant Regency building visible through the arch has been shop-fronted.

Midland Road: W.W.Winter's premises, now colour-washed as pictured in the later 1940s.

Midland Road: a similar scene to one shown earlier except that it was taken about a decade later. The Lancia has given way to a newer car.

Midland Place: Derby Station (Midland Railway) *c.*1890. the interior. The steel and glass roof was destroyed by enemy action in January 1941.

Midland Place: Derby Railway Station (Francis Thompson, 1839) as rebuilt with *porte cochère* in the 1860s by John Sanders. It was again rebuilt in 1897 and demolished in 1982. Photograph *c.*1880.

Midland Place: Derby Railway Station shortly after rebuilding in 1897. The two flanking office buildings were rebuilt to match the new façade. Note the horse tram, left.

Midland Place: Derby Railway Station *c.*1906. The 1897 rebuilding by Charles Trubshaw saw the entire façade expanded forwards to align with the Midland Railway Office building to the left, although the *porte cochère* was retained.

Midland Place: Derby (Midland) Railway Station in the late 1970s, prior to demolition in 1982. The large building (right) is an administrative office of 1862, by John Sanders, and recently saved from demolition.

Midland Place Lounge (now Dining Room) of the Midland Hotel (Francis Thompson, for the Midland Railway, 1839-1841) as redecorated in 1932. By 1935, a barrier had been built, of glass and timber, between the room and the corridor left.

Sturgess & Co delivery wagon at their Canal Street premises in the 1880s.

Normanton Road, looking north *c.*1930. Note the octagonal turret of Rosehill Methodist Church, designed by John Wills, 1874-5, closed 1989 and demolished 1991. Tilling Stevens 'bus of 1931, *en route* for Littleover Lane.

Normanton Road: earlier (c.1907) and further down, a tram bound to Victoria Street picks up a passenger. In the distance, Rosehill Methodist Church; beyond the tram the exotically-shaped tower of Normanton Road Congregational Chapel (T.E.Smith, 1884) which was sold to another sect in the 1960s.

Normanton Road: Alexandra Electric Theatre (converted from an ice-rink to a cinema in 1913) in foreground. It closed in 1953 and was later rebuilt as the Trocadero Ballroom, which was burnt down in 1980. View of *c*.1930.

Arboretum: Derby citizens celebrate a great event, perhaps the 1906 Royal visit.

The Arboretum was England's first public park, given by Joseph Strutt (1765-1844) in 1840 and laid out by John Claudius Loudon (1783-1843). In this 1930s view can be seen, left to right: Lodge (E.B.Lamb, 1840), Orangery (H.Duesbury, 1852), cast-iron fountain (Weatherhead, Glover and Co, 1840) and statue of Sir Henry Royce, Bt, (Derwent Wood, RA, 1933). The latter was later moved to the Riverside Gardens before being transplanted to Rolls Royce's HQ in the 1980s.

Upper Dale Road: St Giles' Garage, pictured in the late 1930s. Note the inexpensive cigarettes available in the dispenser beside the picturesque pumps.

The Spot: 28 June 1906. King Edward VII, having unveiled the statue by C.B.Birch to his mother, prepares to proceed to the Royal Show on Osmaston Park.

Portrait of Edward, Prince of Wales (later King Edward VII) by Winters. This photograph, of which the firm was justly proud, endowed them with Royal patronage: a great boost to trade!

HM Queen Alexandra, wife of Edward VII.

The Spot: left, London Road, right Osmaston Road. The double triumphal arch was erected (largely at the expense of the Mayor, Alderman Sir Alfred Haslam) for Queen Victoria's State Visit of 21st May 1891, a miserably wet day, as this photograph dramatically highlights.

HM Queen Mary pictured outside Rangemoor Hall, Staffs, home of the Bass family (Lords Burton) with members of her entourage and her hosts' family in the 1920s.

Osmaston Hall: King George V (left) and Queen Mary (centre) pictured in the steps of the collapsible pavilion used for the Royal Show at Derby. The event is the opening of the 1921 show on 29 June.

HRH George, Duke of Kent, reviewing troops on The Holmes in 1931.

Market Place: visit of HRH Edward Prince of Wales to Derby on 21 February 1928. He turned up the Ashbourne football in the morning, then arrived to review a guard of honour of ex-servicemen and war veterans in the Market Place at 12.30pm with the Lord Lieutenant (Duke of Devonshire) and the Mayor, Alderman Arthur Sturgess. The character to the left of the Duke (in

overcoat) is Colonel H.M.Haywood, the Chief Constable of the Borough; the Mayor stands behind the Prince, right. Guildhall in the background.

21 February 1928. The Prince of Wales visits the LMS Carriage and Wagon Works in the afternoon.

HRH Princess Elizabeth and her fiancé, HRH Prince Philip of Greece (later HM the Queen and HRH the Duke of Edinburgh) arrive at the Council House 27 June 1947.

Corporation Street on 27 June 1947. HRH Princess Elizabeth, having declared the Council House open, leaves for her next engagement.

Sinfin Lane: Barracks (1877) pictured with elements of the 45/95th Sherwood Foresters Regiment during the South African War, probably prior to departure in 1899.

Midland Road: troops of the 2nd Battalion, Sherwood Foresters, en route for the South African War in 1899. They are being mobbed by an enthusiastic crowd.

German officer as a PoW at Donington Hall, 1914-1918.

German prisoners-of-war (both officers) playing chess at Donington Hall, Leicestershire, during World War One (1914-18). The Hall was adapted as a PoW camp for the duration, having been leased by the War Office from Lord Donington. 'Winters' were asked to photograph the inmates.

Sinfin Lane: the Barracks, built 1877, closed 1963, demolished 1982. Home of the 95th (Derbyshire) Regiment from 1881 and the 3rd Battalion, Sherwood Foresters, (45th/95th) Regiment. The howitzer (right) is a World War One captured Mörser 21cm.

Sherwood Foresters (depôt troops) on parade at the Barracks in 1931. Major R.L.Sherbrooke, DSO, the officer commanding the depôt, is in front.

Review of the men of the Sherwood Foresters (45th/95th) Regiment, c.1930. Sinfin Lane Barracks.

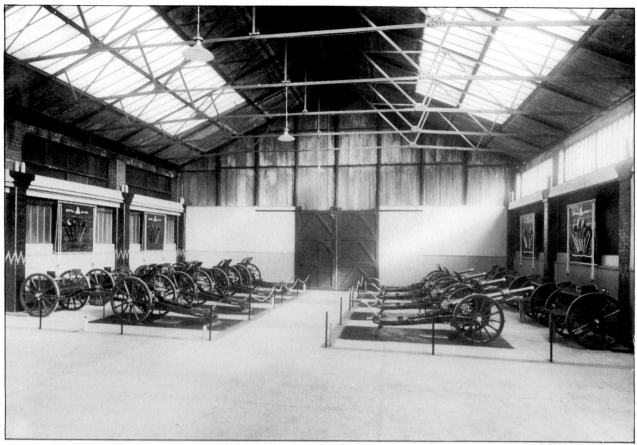

Guns of 246th Field Battery, Royal Artillery, at the Barracks. Probably 1931.

Osmaston Park Road: Guns of 246th Field Battery, Royal Artillery, hitched-up behind their touring vehicles near the Barracks, c.1931.

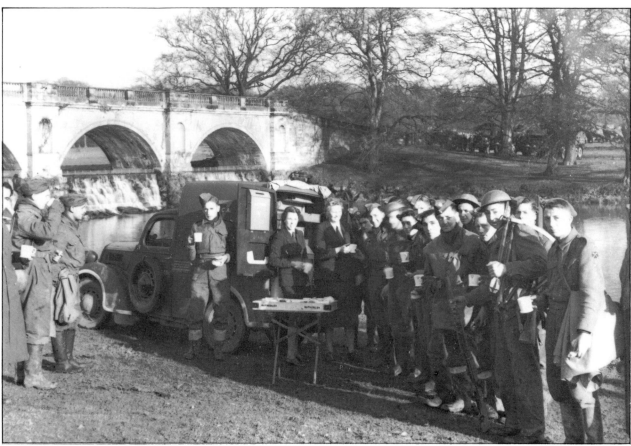

Troops of the 2nd Infantry Division take refreshment in Kedleston Park during World War Two. Note Adam's elegant neo-Classical bridge with its cast-iron balustrade.

Newland Street Dill Hall: the 1935 Trade Fair showing stand of Daltons, leading electrical goods suppliers. Second from left, front row, is a 1935 model Murphy A26 radio, which fixes the approximate date.

Newlands Street Drill Hall. 1935 Trade Fair. Display of Messrs Jay, London Road.

Newlands Street Drill Hall: 1935 trade stand showing Hoover exhibit. This innovative American machine had attracted Royal Warrants from both the King and the Prince of Wales.

Newlands Street Drill Hall: *Derby Daily Telegraph* stand at the trade fair.

Albert Street composing room of the *Derby Daily Express* in the early 1930s.

178 Lucy & Daisy Giuliano
179 D M Higginbottom
180 J W Smith
181 Mrs Margaret Rankin
182 James Mann
183 B J Fleming
184 Reneé Haywood
185 Barrie & Wendy Dunn
186 Barbara Osborne
187 R F Hall
188 David W Slater
189 Mr J W Russell
190 V C Morris
191 Andrew & Rita Harrison
192 Thomas Frederick Stevens
193 Vida Ayres
194 Gerard William McQuillan
195 Alan Sitdown
196 G E Bailey
197 Mrs Marjorie Williams
198 Mr & Mrs P Baines
199 R H & B Vickers
200 Ethel M E Leatherland
201 Phyllis & Martin Du Sautoy
202 Patricia King
203 J I Hall
204 R Williams
205 Jane Steer
206 Mrs G A Faulkner
207 Neville Wild
208 Mr R E Spooner
209 Nicholas Fox
210 Mr Chris Drury
211 Eric Richards
212 David M Pratt
213 L Campbell
214 Les Wilson
215 John M Naden
216 David A Naden
217 Mr J P Rigley
218 T J Larimore
219 R M Larimore
220 Philip Singleton
221 Barry Singleton
222 Anita Maidens
223 M R Bratby
224 Elizabeth Stally
225 Alan Worley
226 Audrey & George Harlow
227 Frederick John Odell
228 Hilda Kent
229 Christopher Shelton
230 Walter Lowe
231 Mrs F Spendlove
232 B R Francis
233 Mrs D Middleton
234 R Sewter
235 Clive J Hobson
236 John M Morris
237 Leonard Matthews
238 K E & L M Chatterley
239 Bernard C Butcher
240 Eric Bennett
241 Malcolm Atkinson
242 R & M Manester
243 Brenda Whelan
244 Jean Hunt
245 George Alan Smith
246 Charles Selby
247 Mrs M G Keys

248 John Smith
249 B E Cash
250 J Kniveton
251 Harold Davis
252 Eric W Chorley
253 Bernard E Brown
254 Jessie Tomlinson
255 Mr & Mrs A V Nixon
256 Thomas William Pearce
257 Mrs Susan Pinchbeck
258 John Bradshaw
259 John Bradshaw
260 J Stallion
261 Phil & Carol Nicklin
262 Mr John Bernard Brittain
         MISM
263 Mrs D West
264 Geoffrey Foggon
265 George Selwood
266 Matthew Wigley
267 Thomas Wigley
268 Dennis Henry Woolliscroft
269 Mr E H & Mrs T Harrison
270 Graham Thompson
271 John L Skidmore
272 C Jones
273 P A Stratton
274 C A Manning
275 Mr K R Rodgers
276 V Matthews
277 Ms Lorraine Garfield
278 George F Young
279 A J Vanter
280 Edward Sandall
281 Miss Pauline A King
282 Mr D A Church
283 Hazel Joyce Buxton
284 K J Yeomans
285 Gordon Gerald Chattle
286 W M Peppiatt
287 Mr R Holyoake
288 Neville Pacey
289 Cyril Laban
290 Dorothy Brodie
291 Anne & Michael Scales
292 A Bird
293 W Renshaw
294 Mr & Mrs G A Chapman
295 Brian & Sarah Chapman
296 P M Caruth
297 Mr G Buxton
298 Mrs Bernadette Webster
299 J Halford
300 Donald Hamilton James
301 Mr & Mrs M W Dallman
302 Terry Goold
303 Tracy Goold
304 H Whittingham
305 C A Whittingham
306 Stephen K Insley
307 M R Beach
308 Patricia A Potts
309 Mrs Grace Pearce
310 John Moxhay
311 Gwen Rickards
312 David A Walker
313 B & G Pritchard
314 J R G Sutcliffe
315 Antony Paul Redfern
316 Ian Potter

317 Mrs Shella Coulthread
318 Stuart Brunyee
319 Joan M Paginton
320 Peter S Hinkley
321 John D Ash
322 P Kirkman
323 Charles Beckett
324 Arthur H Bonser
325 P R Bown
326 Janet Morgan
327 Miss Charlotte Marie Bullock
328 M K Golding
329 L W & V M Gregory
330 J R Cotton
331 Mrs Josephine Hill
332 John & Audrey Shaw
333 John F Gaucher
334 David Oldfield
335 Jeff Topham
336 Les Henshaw
337 James R Freeman
338 James R Freeman
339 David Stanley Page
340 P M Wilton
341 Kenneth Holmes
342 Gordon Tunnicliff
343 Graham E Wells
344 J M Randall
345 W G Heseltine
346 Sheila A Coutts
347 Robert I Bargh
348 Derek J Bargh
349 J H & Mrs S Treece
350 Stuart Cliff
351 Mrs C Gould
352 E West
353 Richard Watson
354 Mr J Calladine
355 Mrs A Pritchard
356 A J Poynton
357 Janet & Denis Bosworth
358 Mr Wilfred Allen
359 Mrs Jean Harrison
360 George Leslie Greem
361 Peter and Noreen Blackwell
362 B R & D Farnsworth
363 Brian Sessions
364 H C Colemman
365 Noel G King
366 S Wilton
367 Fay M Stevenson
368 R G Wheatley
369 A P Northedge
370 John Simpson
371 C H Barrow
372 M Ainsworth
373 Donald A Watkinson
374 Roland G Clewes
375 Thos E Walker
376 B A Lacey
377 Frances E Coulton
378 Fredrick Paul & Sharon Zita
         Milwain
379 Gail Goodman
380 David Widdows
381 Alan A Smith
382 L Douglas Brown
383 Norman Ingman
384 F W Odell
385 D M Learman

386 I Ludlam
387 Mrs Beryl M Mousley
388 Ernest W Hair
389 Lillian McCann
390 D Gardner
391 Antonia Ashmole
392 P S & T Thomas
393 P R Binks
394 J Binks
395 Mrs R L Padmore
396 Donald Anthony Eyden
397 Mr Leonard Walker
398 Thomas E Stanley
399 Dr & Mrs R F Pocock
400 Miss M Campbell Wilson
401 Miss M Campbell Wilson
402 Jonathan Goodall
403 Anthony David Broughton
404 Brian Shaw
405 James Edward Boulter
406 Frank Reader
407 Michael E Briggs
408 Brian Fearn
409 E J Lynch
410 Stephen Wilshaw
411 Mrs Sheila Carrington
412 Mr H J Wallis
413 J Eland
414 G E Mallett
415 D & A McIntosh
416 J A Hedley Snr
417 Olive Allsopp
418 Mr & Mrs C W Hall
419 Derek Limer
420 Roger Pegg
421 Ronald Cooper
422 John Kay
423 Mr E J Alcock
424 Mrs J Keenan
425 Pete Coxon
426 Peter Purnell
427 Edward H Kitchen
428 David J M Lowndes
429 Andrew James Brownson
430 A Spink
431 B Eckersley
432 L Bestwick
433 Alan and Gill Hiley
434 K W Martin
435 Mr R Physick
436 Duncan Benson
437 Ken Miller
438 Joyce M Ramsden
439 Harold S Ayres
440 Barbara Field Dunton
441 Mrs N Alderman
442 Derek and Ann Statham
443 Yvonne McCree
444 B S Morgan
445 B S Morgan
446 David Whittaker
447 R D Taylor
448 J B Lowe
449 R J Whitehurst
450 Kathleen Merry
451 P Gibbons
452 David George Sharp
453 C R Hart
454 R V Birch
455 E V Birch

456 Mrs B D Bates
457 E Wibberley
458 Mrs J J Winfield
459 Eunice Griffiths
460 Ralph Richardson
461 N M & E R Pickford
462 Keith Webb
463 Mrs J M Eason
464 Sheila Redfern
465 K J Guy
466 J C Seaman
467 William Burns
468 Margaret Saville
469 Barbara Coupe
470 Mrs Maureen Cox
471 Kenneth Reader
472 Mrs S V Radford
473 Mr C J Cook
474 Colin J Burford
475 Ivor Mee
476 Mr Michael J F Green
477 Mr John F Raynes
478 Christopher D Kirby
479 Alan Stewart JP
480 Russell George Kinsey
481 W H Allsop
482 John P Bennett
483 Robert W Bestwick
484 Mrs E E Leitch
485 V M Wallbank
486 E J Walters
487 J M Hemingway
488 Sue Shipman
489 Mr William F Bull
490 J E Fearn
491 John Smith
492 Alan Watson
493 B Carpenter
494 H Ireland
495 T M Walsh
496 Frederick Watson
497 C L Major
498 Edward Earley
499 Phyllis E Northcott
500 Sandra & Mick Parkin
501 Mr & Mrs W W Thomson
502 Mr & Mrs I C Thomson
503 Mr K P Fowlkes
504 Alan Cooper
505 Elaine McGiven
506 J Ian Morton
507 Michael McLoughlin
508 J K Braidley
509 David R Long
510 Susan M Brown
511 Chris & Ken Banks
512 Miss B Cunningham
513 Mr & Mrs B Hazlewood
514 H G Oldbury
515 Eric Ronald Foster
516 Gerald Walter Haywood
517 Janet Brocklehurst
518 Eric Buckley
519 J W & E M Lester
520 Ian Brown
521 P O Hutchinson
522 J E J Hutchinson
523 William Keats
524 Dennis Martin
525 Margaret Pearson

526 Margaret Pearson
527 J Savage
528 Carolyn Hardy
529 Anthony Michael Johnson
530 Gordon H Copestake
531 D D Taylor
532 Louis Reader
533 Pam Moss
534 Russell Burke
535 David Sanders
536 John Kingham
537 C A Weightman
538 Bruce Townsend
539 K E Needham
540 Mary Lawrence
541 J Brownsword
542 Brian Knight
543 Richard Andrew Mead
544 Bryan Walkerdine
545 George Edward Rawson
546 Stephen Barnes
547 James McLean
548 Mr G G Wells
549 Pamela Spencer
550 D G Monk
551 William G Plant
552 J D Ash
553 J A Shackleford
554 Steven May
555 B M Bennett
556 Brian Draper
557 R S Brindley
558 Olive E Pritchard
559 Stephen John Boothby
560 John F Challands
561 Reginald J Fentem
562 Raymond Reader
563 R & J Stone
564 Helen & Dave Rigley
565 J LeC Smith
566 A L Allsebrook
567 Joan M Holman
568 David Parry
569 Ian Griffiths
570 Brian E Shuff
571 Glyn Brough
572 Mrs Jean Wells
573 J K Windle
574 Mr & Mrs B Tunnicliffe
575 Iris Stone
576 F R C Salt
577 Mrs O A Wright
578 Jeremiah A Stack
579 Sidney R Jackson
580 Wilfred H Wood
581 John Arguile
582 Mr J E Frith
583 Mary T Longdon
584 Mr & Mrs A W Waldram
585 B J Timbers
586 Beth Johnston
587 Mr A A Taylor
588 Mr & Mrs G Townsend
589 Elizabeth Garrington
590 D S Marsden
591 M Cregan
592 Mr C K Hardy
593 L T Beeston
594 C H Sprenger
595 Mr & Mrs C Edwards

596 Brenda Rutherford
597 P A Maguire
598 Olive Byatt
599 Miss E Naylor
600 Mrs Rose Spiby
601 Alan C Wormald
602 Barry K Edwards
603 Edith Sims
604 Edna Johnson
605 James & Valerie Worsnop
606 Steve Beeson
607 Keith John Siddons
608 Andrew Whyman
609 C G Smith
610 A J Carter
611 Richard Murray
612 Dennis Miller
613 Mark Higginson
614 Mrs Josephine Pewtress
615 Stewart Sillett
616 Alan & Sue Exton
617 Arlette Beverly White
618 Barbara & Geoff Smout
619 Alan Terence Annable
620 Melanie Fowkes
621 W Harper
622 Dennis Vallely
623 Roy Twells
624 Mr & Mrs R S Scattergood
625 Mr & Mrs B Evans
626 G W Moore & W M Blagg
627 Pat & Terry Chell
628 Mr A J Worrall
629 Gerald & Olive Nutty
630 F M Rivett
631 G H Woodings
632 Harry M Gaskill
633 Ann Pether
634 Mick Derby
635 W W Bromley
636 Glenda F Davidson
637 J Murfin
638 A J Regan
639 Mr L Kilbourne
640 D J Millington
641 Mr & Mrs F Record
642 A H Jones
643 Mr & Mrs G E Orchard
644 G B Crooks
645 Jack Slater
646 George Cheetham
647 Hilda D Stone
648 Ernest Howarth
649 Sheila Amin
650 Margaret Jean Pickering
651 Phyllis Nash
652 M Giles
653 Miss F Byrne
654 A Cheetham
655 M C Billings
656 M D Stephenson
657 Jean Ambrose
658 Gordon A Baker
659 Tony Kitchen
660 V M Leveaux
661 Arthur Keetley
662 Derek T Meigh
663 Arnold Woodhouse
664 Mike Barraclough
665 Mr & Mrs P Bilson

666 Peter Fowler
667 Gordon Cooper
668 Bette Cheetham
669 Agnes Ruth Phillips
670 Mr & Mrs F Wilson
671 Alan Whitaker
672 John Raymond Wilson
673 Arthur Bradgate
674 Brian Dale
675 Colin S Bell
676 Robert D Clayborn
677 Mr & Mrs N B Brotherhood
678 Cyril Yeoman
679 Michael Leslie
680 Janice Helen Clark
681 Richard L Knowles
682 M C Dyson
683 Stephanie Elizabeth Martin
684 P S Harland
685 Joyce Baugh
686 Gerald William Brown
687 Ian & Christine Burrows
688 Victor Richard Norvaisa
689 D A & L J Brailsford
690 S J Sharpe
691 Allan Royle
692 Mary Rose
693 Mr Frank Hartshorne
694 Trevor A Grimster
695 P A C Downing
696 George W T Dorrington
697 Jim Haynes
698 M Boardman
699 M Boardman
700 Mr D K Hubbard
701 Dorothy Sharpe
702 Michael John Dunn
703 Norma Consterdine
704 Arthur Woolley
705 D J & A J Meddings
706 J D Norman
707 Mrs D M Dixon
708 J M Thornhill
709 Frank Rodgers
710 Wilfred Holt
711 John W Harrison
712 Dr Fletcher
713 David Wild
714 S A Saxelby
715 Ailsa Schofield
716 Oliver W Eley
717 John Slater
718 Mr & Mrs G Bethell
719 Mr P A Bethell
720 Brian D Bill
721 Brian Allan Reid
722 David Williams
723 Eric A Swales
724 Roger Mather
725 John H Gibson
726 Jill Frawley
727 T W Hall
728 Colin Godfrey
729 Paul Varga
730 Sean P Jeffrey
731 Paul N Fowkes
732 Peter Kite
733 Norman Alec Fenn
734 Antony P Bray
735 Mrs J Butler

736 David Phillips
737 Andrew C Morrell
738 Vincent John Iles
739 Christian Fletcher
740 Cyril James
741 Mr Brian Myring
742 Derek Corbett
743 Arthur Tarr
744 Harry Malcolm Shelley
745 Seamus Bernard Moran
746 Mr R S Smith
747 Joan Lowis
748 Marie Barnes
749 G J Keetley
750 Dennis Smith
751 B Henderson
752 Janet Mitchell
753 E Trelfa
754 Barbara Storey
755 John Adams
756 F R Barker
757 Harold Gray
758 A L Simnett
759 Sheila C Minion
760 Jesse H Booth
761 Marion Johnson
762 Derek Smith
763 Peter Verity
764 David & Nicola Crowther
765 N G Evans
766 Mr Jack Billington
767 G W Beadsmoore
768 F & S Duerden
769 Joan & Ted Phillips
770 Carol Bonsall
771 Richard S Arnold
772 Keith Walkerdine
773 Ruth Braddock
774 Eric Buxton
775 Mr & Mrs R A Shaw
776 Mr J W Shaw
777 Mr G Lyon
778 Mrs C M Sutton
779 Peggy Ann Ward
780 Mr David Parsons
781 T W Evans
782 Ken & Mary Eggleton
783 Bernard Foster
784 Mr & Mrs M G Oakley
785 Mr B G Phillips
786 S M Mitchell
787 S M Mitchell
788 S M Mitchell
789 C A Topley
790 Richard Baker
791 Mr J Otter
792 A J Brownsword
793 Brian Beaver
794 Joanna M Neal
795 W G Lee
796 Barbara Watson
797 Harry Hurst
798 Mr A R Redsell
799 Anthony T Clifton
800 Duncan Mark Chambers
801 Michael Cohen
802 Colin Wardle
803 F C Luscombe
804 P Myott
805 Margaret Hayward

806 J H Derry
807 Brian L Rowe
808 B Mellor
809 Bryan Lowe
810 Mrs M Parker
811 Rebecca Claire Belfield
812 Mrs Pauline Blurton
813 Keith & Brenda Blood
814 Ron & Jean Waterfield
815 Stephen Michael Leahy
816 Mrs Elwyn Kitchen
817 Brian M Gotheridge
818 Mrs Susan Edwards
819 D G Storer
820 Janet Carter
821 Miss P M Blackton
822 D H Phipps
823 Colin Paulin
824 J A Wilkinson
825 Mrs June Lawrence
826 Anne Smith
827 C I Yates
828 E L Northridge
829 Grace Whitby
830 Ivan Hodkinson
831 Michael E Smith
832 Mrs A E Politowski
833 Joyce Coe
834 J Smith
835 D L Crew & Mrs V E Crew
836 G W Harper
837 Mr P M Deacon
838 C Macdonald
839 Pauline Finlay
840 Mr W Wilkinson
841 Mr & Mrs J K Coxon
842 Brenda J Blincow
843 Charles Windridge
844 Nigel J Bailey
845 Mr D J Stirland
846 Pat Wass
847 Margaret McLoughlin
848 Gregory W Bull
849 Edna B Webb
850 Peter M Stanley
851 Mr A G Marchbank
852 Ian Care
853 David Turner
854 Jean Burdekin
855 Robert Patrick Healey
856 Mrs Joan Blackton
857 Roy Harrison
858 Vera & Ken Walton
859 P H & E M Thompson
860 Ian Sherwood
861 Elsie & Tony Claridge
862 Joanna C Spence
863 A R Wareing
864 Jean Sherwood
865 Lee Simpson
866 Peter Leszczyszak
867 Mr Paul Turnbull
868 Mr Joseph Baxter Esq
869 Mr & Mrs P J Davies
870 A J Rawson
871 Arthur Thomas Eley
872 J Gibbons
873 A J Worrall
874 W H Worrall
875 Jenny Pearce

876 Geoffrey Webb
877 Neil Patrick Smith
878 John J Hudson
879 Edward Billings
880 John Franklin
881 Bernard Rhodes
882 Terry R Hall
883 Raymond Barry Furnival
884 Miss D Hackman
885 Mr J Hackman
886 Miss E J Shepherd
887 Muriel Sellors
888 Mr L Thorpe
889 Mr T S Hill
890 Antony Trevor Dunbar
    Atkinson
891 D Botham
892 Mr R D Burley
893 A J Brown
894 Mrs K M Brown
895 Arthur W Kinsey
896 John W & A Hodgkin
897 Mrs M J Tighe
898 Rosa Hancock
899 John & Audrey Trelford
900 Patricia E Parker
901 Sarah A Hopper
902 Sarah A Hopper
903 Ann Swales
904 Dennis P Rawlings
905 V B Smith
906 Sandra N Leese
907 Alison Haywood
908 Mrs Anne Haywood
909 Derbyshire Archaeological
    Society
910 P J Capewell
911 Mr Francis G Wallis
912 G N Davies
913 Mr Ralph Hagger
914 Bob & Joan Richardson
915 Mr J A Snow
916 John E Compton
917 Mr Keith Crabtree
918 Philip Thomas
919 Gordon F Parsons
920 Maureen Edwards
921 P Moore
922 Peter C Barlow
923 Audrey Horsley
924 Alan Darby
925 R A H O'Neal
926 Geoffrey Lee
927 John P Dyson
928 John P Dyson
929 Mrs Joan Hodgkinson
930 P B Neville
931 Gordon N Nadin
932 Mr & Mrs V J Barber
933 Arthur Cawdell
934 Francis Barke
935 R G Kilpatrick
936 Mr Derek Osman
937 Allan L Ball
938 Kevin & Ena Burton
939 Mr & Mrs J F Griffiths
940 Mr D W Gwinnett
941 Patricia Chisnall
942 Kenneth V Gregory
943 C N Wright

944 Mr & Mrs G R Haywood
945 Allan Bate
946 Julie Fletcher
947 C E W Knight
948 Mrs N Doreen Shipton
949 Mr Arthur Corden
950 David & Lesley Austin
951 Oliver Fox
952 Gary Mortimer
953 E Pickstock
954 I Keightley
955 David Henry Worthington
956 Lawrence Lloyd
957 Joey Northover
958 Betty E Rice
959 Dr Derek G Wraith
960 Lindsey Braithwaite
961 David & Jeanette Mitchell
962 Neil & Sandra Ward
963 Mr & Mrs Ian King
964 Mr & Mrs Keith King
965 Mrs Doris King
966 Mr & Mrs G Francis
967 Mr V Barber
968 Mr C Barson
969 K H Eggleton
970 P G Tomlinson
971 D C & J M Boulton
972 Martin Weston King
973 Edwin Walklate
974 R G Roberts
975 W E & P Leeson
976 Michael J Bourne
977 R Irwin
978 Kj
979 James Chapman
980 Ruth James
981 Margaret R Mack
982 Henry Hill
983 Mr & Mrs Fred C Ward
984 H J Eyre
985 D H Eyre
986 J E Eyre
987 A E Hibbs
988 Barbara Smith
989 Wendy & Roger Statham
990 Jean Storey
991 Betty & Michael Clubb
992 Leslie V Smith
993 Miss Freda Smith
994 Philip Rogers
995 G A Tomson
996 Dr R M Edworthy
997 Mr A H Blood
998 Christopher Bennett
999 John Brailsford
1000 Geoff Spacey
1001 Andrew P Spacey
1002 Stuart Rayner
1003 Desmond Parkinson
1004 V J O'Brien
1005 M B & C M Nordemann
1006 G M Nordemann
1007 J Wright
1008 D & F Butler
1009 James Michael Grainger
1010 Barry Iremonger
1011 Mr John Goodman
1012 Mervyn Charles Manning